"The Secret of Getting Ahead is Getting Started"

--

Introduction: The Simple Truth of Progress

Success often seems elusive, reserved for the exceptionally talented or the unusually lucky. But the reality is far simpler. The true secret of getting ahead is simply to get started. Yet, for many, this first step is the hardest. This book is a practical guide to overcoming inertia, embracing action, and continually moving forward toward your dreams. Each chapter reveals a key aspect of beginning your journey and the mindset needed to keep progressing. Let's uncover the power of getting started, one step at a time.

Table of Contents

Chapter 1: The Fear of Starting and How to Overcome It.

Chapter 2: The Psychology of Procrastination: Understanding and Overcoming It.

Chapter 3: Breaking Down Big Goals into Small Steps.

Chapter 4: Setting SMART Goals to Drive Action.

Chapter 5: Developing a Growth Mindset for Continuous Progress.

Chapter 6: Building Habits That Support Your Goals.

Chapter 7: Harnessing the Power of Accountability.

Chapter 8: Embracing the Journey, Not Just the Destination.

Chapter 9: Maintaining Motivation in the Face of Challenges.

Chapter 10: Reflecting, Learning, and Celebrating Starts.

Conclusion: The Journey Continues.

Chapter 1

The Fear of Starting and How to Overcome It

Starting something new can feel overwhelming. Whether it's a new job, launching a project, or beginning a fitness journey, the fear of the unknown often holds us back. This fear, while natural, is frequently based on exaggerated worries about failure, judgment, or discomfort. To overcome this fear, we must first understand it. Fear is the mind's way of protecting us from perceived danger, but in the context of personal growth, it often transforms into a barrier rather than a shield.

The first step in overcoming this fear is to acknowledge it. Recognize that feeling afraid is normal and does not mean you are incapable. Fear is a common human emotion, and experiencing it does not indicate weakness; rather, it shows that you are about to venture into new and unfamiliar territory. Accepting your fear allows you to take control of it instead of letting it control you.

Next, break down the task at hand into smaller, more manageable steps. The key is to start small—choose an action so tiny that it feels almost effortless. For example, if you fear starting a new fitness routine, commit to just five minutes of exercise a day. This small, achievable step
not only makes the larger goal seem less intimidating but also creates momentum. As you continue, these small successes accumulate, boosting your confidence and diminishing the power of fear.

Additionally, it's crucial to change your mind set about fear. Instead of viewing it as a negative force, see it as a sign that you are challenging yourself and stepping out of your comfort zone. Fear can be a powerful motivator when reframed as a catalyst for growth. Remember, every great achievement begins with the decision to try. Don't wait for the fear to disappear; start despite it. With each action you take, fear loses its grip, and progress begins.

Embracing fear as part of the journey rather than a roadblock transforms it from an enemy to an ally. By understanding, acknowledging, and strategically confronting your fears, you unlock the door to personal and professional growth. The path to success -is paved with courage—the courage to begin, even when fear is present.

Raviikant Lall © 2024

Chapter 2

The Psychology of Procrastination: Understanding and Overcoming It

Procrastination is a widespread obstacle to productivity, often preventing us from even getting started. Many people find themselves delaying tasks while waiting for the "perfect" moment—a moment that rarely, if ever, arrives.

Procrastination can arise from various psychological factors, including fear of failure, perfectionism, or feeling overwhelmed by the scope and size of a task. To overcome procrastination, it's crucial to understand these underlying causes and to implement practical strategies to counter them.

One effective technique to combat procrastination is the "two-minute rule." If a task requires less than two minutes to complete, tackle it immediately. This simple rule helps to break the cycle of inertia, allowing you to build momentum through small, manageable actions that gradually foster a habit of productivity. Starting with small wins can create a snowball effect, making larger tasks seem more approachable.

Another powerful strategy is time-blocking, which involves dedicating specific time slots to work exclusively on particular tasks. By creating a structured schedule, you can reduce distractions and generate a sense of urgency and focus, making it easier to initiate and maintain progress. Time-blocking transforms vague intentions into concrete plans, making procrastination less likely.

Visualization techniques can also play a crucial role in overcoming procrastination. Picture yourself successfully completing a task and savoring the sense of achievement that comes with it. Focus on the positive outcomes and benefits of taking action. This mental imagery can serve as a motivating force, helping you to overcome the initial resistance to starting.

It's important to remember that the hardest part of any task is often just beginning. However, once you take that first step, the momentum will build, and the task will start to feel more manageable. The key is to take action, no matter how small, and allow that action to propel you forward.

Chapter 3

Breaking Down Big Goals into Small Steps

Setting big goals can often feel intimidating, leading many to procrastinate or avoid taking action altogether. The key to making significant progress, however, lies in breaking down these large, ambitious goals into smaller, more manageable tasks. This technique, often referred to as "chunking," allows you to turn daunting objectives into achievable steps and provides a clearer path to success. By focusing on smaller, incremental tasks, you can maintain motivation and better track your progress, reducing the sense of being overwhelmed.

The first step in this process is to clearly define your ultimate goal. Be specific about what you want to achieve and why it matters to you. Once you have a clear vision, break your goal down into smaller milestones that can be completed within shorter time frames. For example, if your goal is to write a book, consider dividing it into manageable tasks such as writing one page per day, drafting an outline for each chapter, or setting aside 30 minutes daily to brainstorm ideas. These smaller, actionable steps help build a sense of accomplishment, reinforcing your commitment to the larger objective.

Next, it's essential to prioritize these tasks based on their importance and urgency. Determine which steps will have the greatest impact on your progress and focus on completing them first. This prioritization helps maintain momentum by ensuring that you are consistently moving forward in a meaningful way. Instead of feeling overwhelmed by the entirety of your goal, concentrate on completing one small task at a time. By doing so, you can reduce the anxiety often associated with large projects and create a steady, manageable path toward your desired outcome.

Breaking big goals into small steps also helps to build confidence. Each completed task serves as a building block toward the final objective, proving to yourself that progress is possible and that the goal is within reach. This sense of forward movement is crucial in maintaining motivation, particularly when the overall objective seems far away. By celebrating each small victory, you create a positive feedback loop that encourages continued effort.

Ultimately, the strategy of breaking down big goals into smaller steps is about creating a structured plan that guides you from where you are now to where you want to be. It shifts your focus from the enormity of the end result to the smaller, actionable steps that make up the journey. Remember, every big achievement is made up of many small actions, and by taking one step at a time, you steadily advance toward your goal.

Chapter 4

Setting SMART Goals to Drive Action

Goal setting is a powerful tool for initiating progress, but not all goals are equally effective. To ensure that your goals translate into meaningful achievements, they should be SMART — Specific, Measurable, Achievable, Relevant, and Time-bound.

Specific goals eliminate ambiguity and provide a clear direction. Instead of setting a vague goal like "get fit," define it with precision: "Run 3 kilometers three times a week." When your goals are specific, you know exactly what you need to do to achieve them.

Measurable goals allow you to track your progress and maintain motivation. For example, if your goal is to save money, determine the exact amount you aim to save each month. This way, you can clearly see how close you are to achieving your objective, which keeps you motivated and accountable.

Achievable goals are realistic and within your control, which helps prevent feelings of frustration or failure. Setting goals that are too difficult can lead to discouragement, while realistic goals build confidence and momentum as you make progress.

Relevant goals align with your core values and long-term objectives, ensuring that your efforts are directed towards something that truly matters to you. When your goals are relevant, you are more likely to stay committed and dedicated, knowing that each step you take brings you closer to your larger vision.

Time-bound goals create a sense of urgency, prompting you to take action sooner rather than later. By setting a deadline, you avoid procrastination and maintain a steady pace towards achieving your goal.

By setting SMART goals, you create a strategic roadmap that guides your actions and keeps you on track. Remember, clarity leads to action; the clearer and more specific your goals, the more driven and motivated you will be to achieve them.

Chapter 5

Developing a Growth Mindset for Continuous Progress

A growth mindset — the belief that abilities and intelligence can be developed through dedication, hard work, and learning — is essential for overcoming obstacles and achieving long-term success. This chapter delves into how to cultivate a mindset that embraces challenges as opportunities for growth rather than as threats to be feared or avoided.

Start by reframing your perception of failure. Instead of viewing failure as a negative outcome, see it as valuable feedback and a crucial component of the learning process. Understand that every mistake provides insight into how to improve, and every setback serves as a stepping stone toward future success. This shift in perspective allows you to approach challenges with curiosity and a willingness to learn, rather than with fear or self-doubt.

To cultivate a growth mindset, practice self-compassion and resilience. Recognize that growth is not a linear path and that setbacks are a natural part of progress. Instead of being overly critical of yourself when things don't go as planned, treat yourself with kindness and understanding. This involves acknowledging your efforts, even when the results are not immediately apparent. Celebrate small wins and progress, no matter how minor they may seem; these victories help build confidence and reinforce the belief that you are capable of growth and improvement.

Replace negative self-talk with positive affirmations. When faced with challenges, remind yourself that growth is a journey, not a destination. Statements like "I am capable of learning new things," or "Every effort I make brings me closer to my goal," can shift your mindset from one of limitation to one of potential. These affirmations help create a mental environment where persistence and effort are valued, and where mistakes are viewed as learning opportunities rather than as personal failures.

By adopting a growth mindset, you become more open to trying new things and tackling new challenges, knowing that your abilities are not fixed but can be expanded with effort and time. This mindset empowers you to persevere through difficulties and maintain momentum, understanding that each step forward, no matter how small, is progress in the right direction. It allows you to see challenges as adventures, mistakes as lessons, and success as the cumulative result of consistent effort and learning.

Ultimately, developing a growth mindset lays the foundation for continuous improvement and lifelong learning. It shifts your focus from proving your worth to improving your abilities, creating a more resilient, adaptable, and successful approach to both personal and professional endeavors.

Chapter 6

Building Habits That Support Your Goals

Habits form the bedrock of success. They shape your daily actions and, ultimately, determine whether you are steadily moving toward your goals or unintentionally drifting away from them. This chapter focuses on how to create and sustain habits that align with your objectives, helping you stay on course and achieve long-term success.

Begin by identifying one habit that aligns closely with your goal. The habit should be specific and straightforward to integrate into your daily routine. For example, if your goal is to write a book, start with a simple habit like "write 200 words every day." This small, manageable habit is easy to maintain, making it more likely that you will stick with it over time.

Next, use the habit loop framework: cue, routine, and reward. The cue is a trigger that initiates the habit — it could be a specific time of day, an action, or a location that signals it is time to start your habit. For instance, if your habit is to exercise every morning, your cue might be waking up and putting on your workout clothes.

The routine is the behavior or action you want to perform, such as the act of writing or exercising. The reward is the benefit you receive from completing the habit, which reinforces the behavior and makes it more likely to be repeated. This could be a sense of accomplishment, a mental note of progress, or even a small treat you give yourself.

To effectively build a habit, consistency is crucial. Start with a habit that is small and easy to accomplish to ensure that you can maintain it over time. The goal is to make the habit so manageable that it becomes almost automatic, reducing the mental effort required to perform it. As you become more consistent, gradually increase the habit's complexity or duration to continue challenging yourself without becoming overwhelmed.

Track your progress to stay motivated and accountable. Use a habit tracker, journal, or app to mark each day you successfully stick to your habit. This visual record of your progress can be incredibly motivating, helping you see how far you've come and encouraging you to keep going. Celebrate each day you maintain your habit, no matter how small it may seem. Recognizing and celebrating your progress reinforces the habit and boosts your confidence.

Over time, these small, consistent actions compound into significant progress. Each time you complete the habit, you strengthen the neural pathways associated with it, making it easier to start and continue the next time. This compounding effect demonstrates the power of small, consistent habits: they gradually build momentum and lead to meaningful, lasting change.

By intentionally building habits that support your goals, you create a solid foundation for continuous progress. Remember, habits are not formed overnight; they require patience, commitment, and regular practice. However, with the right approach, you can create habits that help you stay aligned with your goals, making success not just a possibility but an inevitability.

Chapter 7

Harnessing the Power of Accountability

Accountability is a powerful motivator that can significantly enhance your commitment to achieving your goals. When you share your aspirations with others, you create a sense of responsibility and external pressure that encourages you to stay focused and take consistent action. This chapter explores how to harness the power of accountability to ensure you not only get started but also keep going, even when the journey gets tough.

Start by finding an accountability partner — someone who genuinely supports your goals and is willing to help you stay on track. This could be a friend, family member, colleague, or mentor. Share your plans and specific objectives with them, and clearly communicate the steps you intend to take to reach your goals. Set realistic deadlines and establish a schedule for regular check-ins. Knowing that someone else is aware of your progress, or lack thereof, creates a healthy pressure to follow through on your commitments. The desire to avoid disappointing someone else can often be a stronger motivator than merely relying on your internal willpower.

Consider joining groups or communities that share similar goals or interests. Being part of a community of like-minded individuals provides a built-in network of support, inspiration, and encouragement. These groups can offer valuable feedback, share strategies, and celebrate successes, all of which can boost your motivation and help you overcome obstacles. In addition, observing the progress of others can inspire you to push yourself further and stay committed to your path. Whether it's an online forum, a local club, or a professional network, being surrounded by people who understand your journey can make a significant difference.

Another effective strategy is to publicly commit to your goals. This could involve sharing your intentions on social media, in a blog, or even at a workplace meeting. Public commitments increase the stakes, as more people become aware of your goals and may periodically ask about your progress. This broader sense of accountability can provide an additional layer of motivation, encouraging you to maintain your efforts and stay focused.

Accountability also involves being honest with yourself. Reflect regularly on your progress and assess whether you are moving closer to your goals or getting sidetracked. Use these reflections to make necessary adjustments, recalibrate your efforts, and refine your strategies. Keeping a journal or using a tracking app can help you stay aware of your achievements and areas where you need to improve.

By leveraging the power of accountability, you create an environment that supports your success. You are less likely to procrastinate, make excuses, or give up when you know others are invested in your progress. Remember, accountability is not just about external pressure — it also fosters a deeper commitment to yourself and your dreams. When you know others are watching and rooting for you, you are more likely to rise to the occasion and achieve the goals you have set.

Ultimately, accountability can transform your journey. It transforms your aspirations into shared commitments, ensuring you are not alone in your pursuit of success. With the right support, you will find the strength and motivation to keep moving forward, no matter the challenges that come your way.

Chapter 8

Embracing the Journey, Not Just the Destination

In our pursuit of success, we often become so fixated on the end goal that we overlook the value of the journey itself. While having a clear destination is important, it's equally essential to find joy in the process of getting started and making progress. This chapter encourages you to embrace the journey, savor the small victories, and learn from the lessons that unfold along the way.

When you shift your focus from the destination to the process, you create a more sustainable and fulfilling approach to achieving your objectives. It's important to recognize that every step you take, no matter how small, contributes to your overall growth and success. By paying attention to the journey, you learn to appreciate the incremental progress and the personal development that occurs in the pursuit of your goals.

Learning to celebrate small victories is crucial for maintaining motivation and momentum. These achievements, however minor they may seem, serve as building blocks that move you closer to your ultimate goal. Whether it's finishing a chapter of a book, mastering a new skill, or simply sticking to a daily habit, each small win deserves recognition and celebration. By acknowledging these moments, you reinforce positive behaviors and create a sense of accomplishment that fuels further progress.

Additionally, embracing the journey involves being open to the lessons learned along the way. Not every step will be smooth, and setbacks are inevitable. However, these challenges provide valuable opportunities for growth and self-discovery. Instead of becoming discouraged by obstacles, view them as learning experiences that help you become more resilient, adaptable, and better prepared for future challenges. The journey becomes a classroom where you gain wisdom, refine your skills, and build the strength needed to reach your destination.

Staying present in the journey also helps you manage stress and prevent burnout. When you are overly focused on the end result, you may feel overwhelmed by the gap between where you are and where you want to be. This can lead to frustration, impatience, and even a sense of failure. By grounding yourself in the present moment, you learn to enjoy the process itself, finding satisfaction in the effort rather than just the outcome. This mindset fosters patience, perseverance, and a deeper connection to your goals.

Understand that the journey is where the true transformation happens. It is where you discover your strengths, confront your weaknesses, and develop the character and resilience necessary to achieve lasting success. By embracing the journey, you not only make the path to your goals more enjoyable, but you also cultivate a mindset that values growth, learning, and progress in all aspects of life.

Remember, success is not just about reaching the destination — it's about who you become along the way. When you find joy in the process, every step becomes meaningful, every challenge becomes an opportunity, and every moment brings you closer to becoming the best version of yourself. Embrace the journey, and the destination will take care of itself.

Chapter 9

Maintaining Motivation in the Face of Challenges

Challenges are an inevitable part of any worthwhile journey, but how you respond to these obstacles ultimately determines your success. Staying motivated when difficulties arise is crucial to keeping you on track toward your goals. This chapter provides practical strategies to help you maintain motivation, even in the face of setbacks and adversity.

One effective way to sustain motivation is by setting mini-goals. Breaking down your larger objectives into smaller, manageable tasks allows you to create a series of quick wins that keep your spirits high. Each mini-goal you accomplish brings a sense of achievement and builds momentum, making it easier to stay focused and motivated. These smaller milestones help you see progress more clearly, reinforcing the belief that you are moving forward, even if the end goal still seems distant.

Another key strategy is to establish a routine that fosters consistency. Consistency is often more powerful than motivation alone because it creates habits that carry you through moments when motivation naturally wanes. Design a daily or weekly schedule that includes specific times for working on your goals. By turning your goals into a regular practice, you reduce reliance on fleeting feelings of motivation and build a disciplined approach that keeps you moving forward regardless of how you feel on any given day.

When you find your motivation fading, revisit your "why." Remind yourself of the reasons you started this journey and the specific goals you hope to achieve. Reflect on the deeper purpose behind your ambitions, whether it's personal growth, financial stability, helping others, or fulfilling a lifelong dream. Connecting with your core motivations can reignite your passion and renew your commitment, providing a strong anchor when faced with doubts or difficulties.

Seek inspiration from others who have overcome similar obstacles. Read books, listen to podcasts, or watch videos featuring people who have faced and conquered challenges like yours. Surrounding yourself with stories of resilience and perseverance can remind you that you are not alone and that success is possible despite the odds. Learning from others' experiences can also offer new strategies and perspectives to help you overcome your own hurdles.

Remember that motivation is not always a feeling; it's a choice. On days when motivation feels elusive, make a conscious decision to stay committed to your goals. Understand that motivation can ebb and flow, but commitment is a constant that you control. Choose to take action, even if it feels challenging or inconvenient. Often, motivation returns once you begin moving forward again, proving that progress can be the best remedy for a lack of inspiration.

In summary, maintaining motivation in the face of challenges requires a combination of practical strategies and a resilient mindset. By setting mini-goals, establishing a consistent routine, reconnecting with your "why," and seeking inspiration from others, you equip yourself with the tools to stay motivated even when the path is difficult. Remember, staying motivated is not just about feeling inspired; it's about making a conscious decision to keep going, no matter what.

By choosing to remain committed to your goals, you cultivate the strength and perseverance needed to achieve lasting success.

Chapter 10

Reflecting, Learning, and Celebrating Your Starts

Reflection is a powerful tool for personal and professional growth. In this final chapter, we emphasize the importance of taking time to reflect on your progress, learning from your experiences, and celebrating each new beginning. Recognize that every start, no matter how small, is a victory in itself and brings you one step closer to your dreams.

Start by taking time to reflect on your journey. Regular reflection allows you to evaluate what strategies worked well and what didn't, helping you to identify areas for improvement. Consider setting aside time each week or month to assess your progress. Ask yourself questions such as: What have I accomplished? What challenges have I faced, and how did I handle them? What could I have done differently? This process helps you gain valuable insights into your actions and decisions, enabling you to adjust your approach and continue moving forward with greater clarity and purpose.

Learning from your experiences is key to continuous growth. View every step, success, and setback as an opportunity to gain knowledge and develop resilience. Mistakes and failures are not indicators of your limitations; they are essential parts of your journey that offer valuable lessons. Embrace these lessons with a growth mindset, understanding that each experience equips you with the skills and wisdom needed for future success. By learning from both your achievements and your setbacks, you build a stronger foundation for your next steps.

Celebrate each start and every step forward, no matter how small. Recognizing and celebrating your efforts reinforces positive behavior and motivation, making it easier to stay committed to your goals. Celebrate not only the big milestones but also the small victories along the way — finishing a task, overcoming a fear, or simply beginning something new. Each start is a courageous step toward your aspirations and deserves to be acknowledged. This celebration fosters a sense of accomplishment and keeps you motivated to keep moving forward.

Remember that starting is a victory in itself. The act of beginning, of taking that first step, is often the hardest part. Each new beginning brings you closer to your dreams, and the courage to start again and again, despite the challenges, is what ultimately leads to success. Don't be afraid to start over; every fresh start provides a chance to apply what you've learned, to approach your goals with renewed energy, and to build on the progress you've already made.

The secret to getting ahead is not about starting just once; it's about being willing to start over and over again, each time with renewed determination and enthusiasm. Understand that progress is not always linear. There will be times when you need to pause, regroup, and begin anew. This is not a sign of failure but of resilience and commitment to your vision.

In conclusion, reflection, learning, and celebration are essential components of your journey to success. Embrace each new beginning as an opportunity for growth. Celebrate every step, learn from every experience, and use each start as a foundation for future progress. Remember, success is not defined by how many times you reach the finish line, but by how often you dare to begin again.

Conclusion

The Journey Continues

The journey to success is not a straight path; it is a series of starts, stops, and restarts. It is filled with moments of progress, setbacks, learning, and growth. Each step forward, no matter how small, is a victory in its own right, and every new beginning brings you closer to achieving your dreams. The most important thing is to keep moving, to keep starting anew, and to never lose sight of your aspirations.

Understand that success is not defined by a single achievement or a final destination; it is a continuous process of growth and self-discovery. Every challenge you face, every obstacle you overcome, and every fresh start you make is a crucial part of this process. Rather than being discouraged by the twists and turns of your journey, embrace them as opportunities to learn, to adapt, and to strengthen your resolve.

So, take that first step today — no matter how uncertain or small it may feel. Trust in the process and believe in your ability to make progress, one step at a time. Remember that the secret to getting ahead is not just in dreaming big, but in having the courage to begin, and the determination to keep going, even when the road gets tough.

The journey to success is ongoing. It evolves as you do, with each new goal, each new challenge, and each new beginning. Keep starting, keep striving, and keep moving forward. With every step, you are writing your own story of success, one that is unique, meaningful, and entirely yours.

And remember — the secret to getting ahead is simple: just get started, and keep starting, again and again.

www.ingramcontent.com/pod-product-compliance
Lightning Source LLC
Chambersburg PA
CBHW062238220526
45471CB00009B/3531